# MockTales

# MockTales

## 50+ LITERARY MOCKTAILS

### Inspired by Classic Works, Banned Books, and More

Delanie Fischer
Lindsey Smith

MIAMI

Cover Design: Lucy Giller
Cover Photo/illustration: Lucy Giller
Layout & Design: Lucy Giller

For permission requests, please contact the publisher at:
Mango Publishing Group
5966 South Dixie Highway, Suite 300
Miami, FL 33143
info@mango.bz

For special orders, quantity sales, course adoptions and corporate sales, please email the publisher at sales@mango.bz. For trade and wholesale sales, please contact Ingram Publisher Services at customer.service@ ingramcontent.com or +1.800.509.4887.

MockTales: 50+ Literary Mocktails Inspired by Classic Works, Banned Books, and More

Library of Congress Cataloging-in-Publication number: 2024946776
ISBN: (print) 978-1-68481-709-2, (ebook) 978-1-68481-710-8
BISAC category code: CKB008000, COOKING / Beverages / Non-Alcoholic

Cheers to sharing great drinks
and even better stories.

# Introduction

# Set the Scene

# The Classics

# Banned Books

# Book-to-Movie Adaptations 91

# Book Clubs 123

# The Sober Games 139

# Conclusion 143

# Acknowledgments 144

# About the Authors 145

# Introduction

Ernest Hemingway famously said, "Write drunk, edit sober."

*Or did he?*

Nope! That's an apocryphal quote—in reality, Hemingway rarely drank while writing, preferring to keep business and pleasure separate. Even Papa Hemingway, infamous boozer and cat daddy, knew that a clear head (and a cat) was a key part of becoming a literary icon.

*MockTales* mixes up alcohol-free drinks with the characters, settings, and vibes of timeless books to gin up the perfect booze-less pairings.

Have you ever wondered what Elinor and Marianne, from Jane Austen's novel *Sense & Sensibility*, would sip on the chilly evenings in Barton Cottage? Try a **Soda & Sensibility**. This drink combines Elinor's romantic sense (cranberry, orange, and lemon) with Marianne's more medicinal sensibility (agave and mint).

If adventure fiction like Paulo Coelho's *The Alchemist* is more your speed, then you'll enjoy sipping on **The Nonalcoholic Alchemist Elixir** while you plan your next escapade. This magical elixir combines the tart and tang of citrus with the sweetness of pineapple, capturing the ebbs and flows of life's journey.

While you might not be hitting the sauce as hard as Dorothy Parker ("Three be the things I shall never attain: Envy, content, and sufficient champagne") or F. Scott Fitzgerald ("Too much of anything is bad, but too much champagne is just right"), you can still bask in their literary genius and party in their honor—without the hangover.

Grab one of these mocktails as you settle in with your favorite read.

# Set the Scene

Let's set the scene! This is where you'll get familiar with the tools and alcohol-free swaps needed to begin creating your very own mocktail.

## Tools to Kill a Mocktail

**Knife**—or an 1800s cast iron food chopper, if you're in your Dickens era

**Muddler**—or a 1900s wooden potato masher, if you wanna get your Hemingway on

**Shaker**—or your favorite 1920s hand mixer

**Vegetable peeler or paring knife**—
or a bow-bread knife, if you happen
to be a great baker like Virginia

**Pitcher**—or dust off your
cobalt blue, ivy-decorated
ceramic water jug

**Teapot**—or an open flame and whatever-
sized copper pot you may have lying
around your public room, hall, or chamber

**A variety of drinking glasses**—
or your favorite iron and brass
ladles

**Fun-shaped ice cube molds**—
or literal balls of snow

# Goblets, Gimlets, and Glassware–Oh My!

**COLLINS/HIGHBALL GLASS**

**COUPE GLASS**

**DELMONICO GLASS**

**FLUTE**

**GIMLET GLASS**

**GOBLET**

**GRAPPA GLASS**

**HURRICANE GLASS**

**MARGARITA GLASS**

**MARTINI GLASS**

**MULE MUG**

**SHOOTER GLASS**

**ROCKS GLASS**

**RED WINE GLASS**

**SHOT GLASS**

**SNIFTER**

**WHITE WINE GLASS**

# Plot Twist:
# Fyodor's (Alcohol-Free) Flavor Swaps

With the rise of alcohol-free living, there are now many brands that have perfected alcohol-free swaps that taste like the real thing. Those are great substitutes for things like gin, vodka, and other alcohols that have more complex profiles, for when you are craving that specific taste.

However, you might not have access to those substitutes regularly, so we put together a chart to help you find similar tastes with ingredients you likely have at home.

| Type of Alcohol | Substitutes |
|---|---|
| **Amaretto** | Almond extract or Italian soda syrup |
| **Bourbon** | 1 tsp vanilla extract |
| **Brandy** | Unsweetened orange or apple juice, plus 1 tsp vanilla extract |
| **Champagne** | Sparkling white grape juice or sparkling apple cider |
| **Coffee liqueur** | 1 tsp instant coffee dissolved in water |
| **Cognac** | Apricot, pear, or peach juices |

| | |
|---|---|
| **Creme de cacao** | 1 tsp raw cacao and 1 tsp powdered sugar mixed with 1 Tbsp water |
| **Creme de menthe** | ½ tsp mint extract |
| **Framboise** | Raspberry juice, raspberry syrup, or raspberry jam |
| **Hard cider** | Apple cider |
| **Rum** | Pineapple juice, rum extract, or black tea |
| **Sake** | Rice vinegar |
| **Tequila** | Cactus juice or nectar |
| **Triple sec** | Orange juice or marmalade |
| **Vermouth** | White wine vinegar or white grape juice |
| **Whiskey** | Apple cider with lime juice |
| **Vodka** | Apple cider with lime juice |
| **Wine (dry)** | White grape juice or apple cider with a Tbsp of white vinegar to cut sweetness |
| **Wine (sweet)** | White grape juice or apple cider |
| **Wine (red)** | Grape juice, cranberry juice, and hibiscus tea |

# The Great Garnish–and Other Techniques

## Garnishing

Just like a well-designed book cover, a well-garnished drink can entice, inspire, and turn into an impromptu photo-op for the 'gram. Here are some simple ways to elevate your final draft!

### *Fruits, Flowers, and Fresh Herbs*

You can use a cookie cutter to create fun-shaped fruits to skewer across your glass, drop inside your drink, or perfectly place on the rim by carving a small slice into the shaped fruit.

Whether fresh, dried, or pressed, ensure your flower is edible (soaked in water, gently patted dry) before adding to your drink. This garnish is easy, since it's nearly impossible for a flower to look bad, no matter the placement—just as it was impossible for Toni Morrison to write a bad book. Lay the flower across a glass, rest it on the ice in your drink, or sprinkle your entire table (or bedroom... wink, wink) with rose petals as you present the drink to a special guest.

As with flowers, it's hard to go wrong when you garnish a drink with herbs. However, no matter what herb you use, be sure to give it a slap before placing it in, or around, your drink to release its oil and aroma for an optimal drinking experience that delights all the senses.

### The Twist

An unexpected plot twist can leave us so surprised that we can't put a book down—and a citrus twist is no different. After taking a sip, you won't want to put your drink down.

Here are two easy ways to make a twist to remember. First, using a vegetable peeler, peel a strip of the citrus skin. Give the peel a twist and either drop it in your drink or place it on the edge of your glass. Another way is to cut a slice of fruit with a paring knife (cut along the edge of the peel to remove the pulpy part) and make a slit on one end of the circular peel, twist it around a chopstick or straw, and add to your drink or glass! Whatever tool you use, feel free to clean up any peel that may be rough around the edges, using a small knife.

### Wheel & Wedge

A circular ending in writing finishes the same way a story starts, giving the reader a chance to reflect: Are things the same for the characters or not? The cyclical structure of the citrus wheel can do the same. Is it foreshadowing the flavors of your drink, or is it completely different?

To make a wheel, chop the fruit in half and cut a slice. Create a slit from the center of the wheel to the edge; this will allow you to slide it onto the rim of your glass.

For a wedge, trim the ends of the fruit, cut the fruit in half lengthwise, remove the pith (writing can be pithy, fruit

can be pithy, fun right?), and cut the fruit into wedges. Make a slit in the wedge to dress up the side of your glass, or drop the wedge into the drink for some added flavor.

**Hot tip:** Slice up some starfruit for an instant, fun-shaped wedge!

### *Fun Finishes*

Use all the above techniques on anything else you want: olives, cinnamon sticks, an entire burger. Plus, don't forget sprinkles, shavings, candy, zest, and cool-lookin' ice cubes are quick and easy ways to spruce up a drink!

## Muddling

Maybe you reread your favorite book to savor each moment and extract every possible life lesson from it. Muddling is no different. You're squeezing every ounce of juice, oil, and flavor out of the ingredients so you can savor every delicious sip.

Add the ingredients to a sturdy glass, press down, and twist with your muddler until everything is, well, muddled. Be gentle with herbs—they only need a little push to release their oils and aromas. Pressing them too hard can leave a bad taste in your mouth, like someone ripping out the very last page of your book, leaving you to never know how it ends.

## Shaking

Sometimes, authors have to shake things up to keep their readers engaged, and sometimes you have to shake things up to keep your drinks interesting. You'll be shaking some ingredients when you need to achieve a chilled drink or a smooth texture, or to awaken flavors.

Add the ingredients to a shaker, shake back and forth several times, and strain into a glass.

Just don't shake any carbonated liquids, unless you want a cold mess on your hands. You'll add the fizzy ingredients directly to the glass.

## Rimming

A delicious rim is like a good logline of a book. It gives you a little taste before diving into the main event.

Whether it's salt, sugar, spices, zest, chocolate, or any other magical ingredient, rimming a glass is a piece of cake. Oh my gosh, can you rim a glass with cake? Yes. The answer is always yes.

Spread some of the rimming ingredients onto a plate. Wet the rim with a citrus wedge, syrup, or water; feel free to use a liquid that's found in a recipe or use something that complements it. Turn the glass upside down and dip the rim into the ingredients.

For a more unique look, wet, and dip, any edge of the glass—it doesn't have to be the rim!

## Stirring

This one is self-explanatory, like enjoying a picture book.

When a recipe calls for a stir to combine the ingredients, stir the drink for about 30 seconds or so, in a circular motion.

However, when adding a carbonated liquid, one or two stirs will suffice. We don't want that fabulous drink to fall flat, like the ending of *Huckleberry Finn*.

# Simple Syrups of Endearment

Disgrace abounds, but good simple syrups are rare. These simple syrups can be used for any mood and occasion.

## Classic Simple Syrup

**INGREDIENTS**

1 cup water

1 cup granulated sugar

**INSTRUCTIONS**

1. In a small saucepan, combine water and sugar.

2. Over medium heat, stir until sugar has completely dissolved.

3. Let cool and refrigerate in a glass jar.

**Note:** Build upon the story! You can infuse almost any flavor into the classic simple syrup. You can play with the type of sugar, the water ratio, and the flavor profile. Experiment and get creative. Think of it as a first draft that you can edit as needed.

# Lavender Syrup

## INGREDIENTS

1 cup water

1 cup granulated sugar

2 Tbsp dried culinary lavender buds

1 tsp butterfly pea flower tea

## INSTRUCTIONS

1. In a small saucepan, combine water and sugar.

2. Over medium heat, stir until sugar has completely dissolved.

3. Add dried lavender buds and butterfly pea flower to the sugar-water mixture.

4. Let the mixture simmer gently for 5 minutes, then remove from the heat.

5. Allow the lavender to steep in the syrup until it cools to room temperature.

6. Once cooled, strain the syrup to remove the lavender buds and transfer to a clean, airtight container. Refrigerate for up to two weeks.


# Cinnamon Syrup

## INGREDIENTS

1 cup water

1 cup granulated sugar

6–8 cinnamon sticks

## INSTRUCTIONS

1. In a small saucepan, combine water and sugar.

2. Over medium heat, stir until sugar has completely dissolved.

3. Once cool, put the syrup and cinnamon sticks in a glass jar and refrigerate for 24 hours.

4. Remove the cinnamon sticks and serve.

# Vanilla Syrup

## INGREDIENTS

1 cup water

1 cup granulated sugar

1 vanilla bean

## INSTRUCTIONS

1. In a small saucepan, combine water, sugar, and vanilla bean.
2. Over medium heat, stir until sugar has completely dissolved.
3. Strain the syrup, let cool, and refrigerate in a glass jar.

# Berry Syrup

## INGREDIENTS

1 cup water

1 cup granulated sugar

2 cups berries of your choice

## INSTRUCTIONS

1. In a small saucepan, combine water, sugar, and berries.
2. Over medium heat, mix and mash berries.
3. Boil for 3 minutes, or until mixture thickens.
4. Strain into a jar and serve immediately, or store in the fridge for five to seven days.

# MockTales

Just like your favorite authors infuse creativity into their books, you're encouraged to do that with these drinks. We provide guidelines, but you're the writer of your own story. Frankenstein created a memorable monster, and you can do the same with a mocktail.

# The Classics

Your favorite literary classics paired with your favorite classic drinks. These are the ones you'll want to return to again and again.

# The Woman Warrior Ward 8

## *THE WOMAN WARRIOR* BY MAXINE HONG KINGSTON

Warrior women get things done. They become legends offering (sage) advice. And legend has it that the traditional Ward 8 was created on the eve of a Bostonian election in, you guessed it, Ward 8. Ah, but there's an (orange) twist! The famous drink was never tasted by the person it was created for, as they themselves did not drink. This version, however, can be enjoyed by all.

## INGREDIENTS

¾ oz fresh lemon juice

¾ oz fresh orange juice

½ oz grenadine syrup

3 sage sprigs

Soda water or soda water

Ice cubes

Orange twist for garnish (optional)

## INSTRUCTIONS

1. In a cocktail shaker or sturdy glass, muddle fresh lemon juice and fresh sage leaves together until well mashed.

2. Add ice, fresh orange juice, and grenadine syrup to the shaker.

3. Shake well until the mixture is thoroughly chilled.

4. Strain the mixture into a chilled cocktail glass or a rocks glass filled with ice.

5. Add soda water to top it off.

6. Garnish with an orange twist and enjoy!

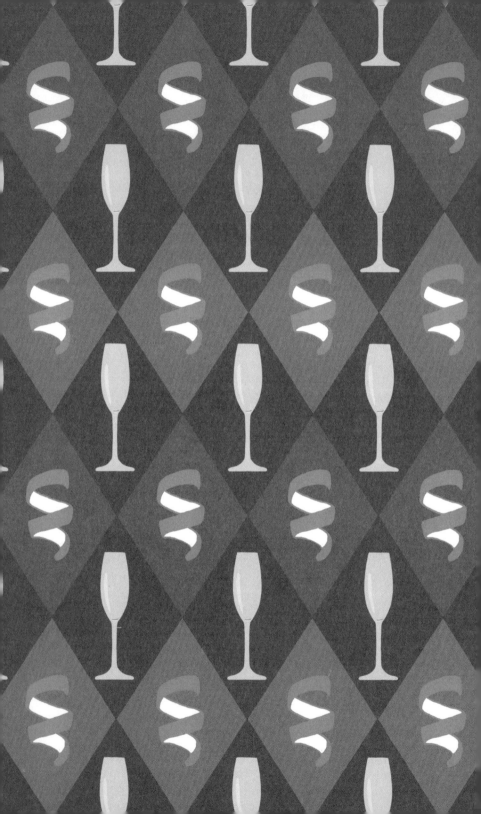

# Go Tell It on the Mimosa

*GO TELL IT ON THE MOUNTAIN* BY JAMES BALDWIN

James Baldwin's semi-autobiographical *Go Tell It on the Mountain* is a classic that explores religion, identity, and family. This twist on another classic is the brunch beverage of choice to have in hand when discussing those complex topics and more with your besties at brunch on Sunday (or any day).

## INGREDIENTS

3 oz orange juice

3 oz soda water or soda water

½ oz fresh lemon juice

Ice cubes

Orange slice or twist for garnish

## INSTRUCTIONS

1. Fill a glass with ice cubes.

2. Pour the orange juice and soda water (or soda water) into the glass.

3. Add the fresh lemon juice if using.

4. Stir gently to combine.

5. Garnish with an orange slice or twist and enjoy!

# Miss Marple's Mule

## *THE MURDER AT THE VICARAGE* BY AGATHA CHRISTIE

Agatha Christie's beloved detective, Miss Jane Marple, made her first appearance in *The Murder at the Vicarage*. In it, Miss Marple of St. Mary Mead muses on marmalade. This seemingly mundane, though marvelous, ingredient finds itself in the delicious Miss Marple's Mule. One sip and it will be no mystery why it's a main character at any event.

### INGREDIENTS

**4 oz ginger beer**

**1 oz fresh lime juice**

**½ oz marmalade**

**Ice cubes**

**Lime wedge or wheel for garnish**

**Fresh mint leaves for garnish**

### INSTRUCTIONS

1. In a shaker or mixing glass, combine the fresh lime juice and marmalade.

2. Stir or shake well to dissolve the marmalade into the lime juice.

3. Fill a copper mug or glass with ice cubes.

4. Pour the lime juice and marmalade mixture over the ice.

5. Top up with ginger beer.

6. Stir gently to mix the ingredients.

7. Garnish with a lime wheel or wedge and fresh mint leaves if desired.

# The Bell Jam Jar

*THE BELL JAR* BY SYLVIA PLATH

There are many things of note from the 1950s and early '60s, to be sure—including the incomparable Sylvia Plath and an entire generation's fascination with fruit-laden treats. This delight is one that cannot be contained. When the lid pops off the Bell Jam Jar, sweet apricot jam coupled with fizzy sparkling soda can effectively melt away any mental cobwebs. Go ahead, have two.

## INGREDIENTS

2 Tbsp apricot jam

½ oz (15ml) fresh lemon juice

1 cup soda water or soda water

Ice cubes

Fresh apricot slice for garnish

## INSTRUCTIONS

1. In a jam jar or glass, add the apricot jam.

2. Pour fresh lemon juice into the jar.

3. Use a spoon or muddler to muddle the apricot jam and lemon juice together until well combined.

4. Fill the jar with ice cubes.

5. Slowly pour soda water or soda water into the jar, stirring gently to mix the ingredients.

6. Garnish with a fresh apricot slice.

# The Non-Alc-Hemist Elixir

*THE ALCHEMIST* BY PAULO COELHO

The pursuit of your life's purpose is full of various ups and downs. In Santiago's case, he encountered many hardships and personal doubts. However, he also experienced moments of beauty and a deep trust in the Universe.

This elixir provides a combination of flavors—the tart and tang of the citrus with the floral notes of the lavender syrup—capturing the essence of the ebbs and flows of life's journey. The addition of ginger ale or soda water provides effervescence, symbolizing the transformative and uplifting qualities your journey to self-discovery can take you on.

## INGREDIENTS

**1 oz fresh lemon juice**

**1 oz fresh orange juice**

**1 oz lavender syrup (see page 21)**

**Ginger ale or soda water**

**Ice cubes**

**Lemon twist or mint sprig (for garnish)**

## INSTRUCTIONS

1. Prepare the lavender syrup using the instructions provided on page 21.

2. In a shaker, combine ice, lemon juice, orange juice, and lavender syrup.

3. Shake well to blend the ingredients.

4. Fill a glass with ice cubes and pour the mixture into the glass, leaving some space at the top.

5. Top off the glass with ginger ale or soda water, depending on your preference. You can adjust the amount to achieve your desired levels of sweetness and fizziness.

6. Garnish and enjoy!

# Mrs. Dalloway's Gâteau de Pommes Daiquiri

## MRS. DALLOWAY BY VIRGINIA WOOLF

~~~~~~~~~~~~~~~~~~~~~~~~~~~~~~~~~~~~~~~~~~~~

Clarissa Dalloway wields social status and elegance effortlessly, leaving no detail to chance. Just as she prepared for a decadent evening being the apple of her guests' eyes, this apple-cake-inspired daiquiri will be sure to do the same for you. Don't let its simplicity fool you. Any guest with refined tastes, as well as yourself, will be impressed by the subtle sophistication this drink brings to the party.

~~~~~~~~~~~~~~~~~~~~~~~~~~~~~~~~~~~~~~~~~~~~

### INGREDIENTS

**2 oz apple juice or apple cider**

**1 oz fresh lime juice**

**½ oz simple syrup (see page 20)**

**Dash of cinnamon**

**Ice cubes**

**Cinnamon stick for garnish**

### INSTRUCTIONS

1. In a shaker, combine the apple juice or cider, fresh lime juice, simple syrup, and a dash of cinnamon.

2. Add ice cubes to the shaker.

3. Shake well until the mixture is thoroughly chilled.

4. Strain the mixture into a glass filled with ice cubes.

5. Garnish with an apple slice or a cinnamon stick if desired.

# There There No-Quila Margarita

## *THERE THERE* BY TOMMY ORANGE

Tommy Orange's debut novel, *There There*, is a poignant portrayal of the struggles and resilience of twelve urban Native Americans on Ohlone land (Oakland, California). Orange juice is featured in this spin on the margarita as a tribute to the author and the contemporary Native experience.

### INGREDIENTS

2 oz fresh lime juice

1 oz fresh orange juice

1 oz agave syrup

½ oz lime cordial

Salt (for rimming the glass)

Lime wedge (for garnish)

Ice cubes

### INSTRUCTIONS

1. Rim a margarita glass with salt by running a lime wedge around the rim and dipping it into a plate of salt.

2. Fill the glass with ice cubes.

3. In a shaker, combine lime juice, orange juice, agave syrup, and lime cordial.

4. Shake well and then strain the mixture into the prepared glass.

5. Garnish the glass with a lime wedge.

# House Made of Dark 'n' Stormy

*HOUSE MADE OF DAWN* BY N. SCOTT MOMADAY

Just as Pulitzer Prize winner, artist, and English professor Momaday expressed himself in many ways—through photography, poetry, painting, and storytelling—this drink combines a variety of potent ingredients that tickle your palate (pun intended).

Inspired by Momaday's reference to "dark infinity" and the contrast to his versatile, colorful art, this bold drink manages to be dark, yet vibrant. Drink in the masterpiece!

## INGREDIENTS

½ cup ice

2 oz freshly squeezed lime juice

1 tsp maple syrup

½ cup ginger beer

Lime wheel for garnish

## INSTRUCTIONS

1. In a shaker, combine ice, lime juice, and maple syrup.

2. Shake until the maple syrup is dissolved.

3. Fill a glass with ice.

4. Strain the mixture over the ice cubes into the glass.

5. Top with the ginger beer.

6. Garnish the glass with a lime wheel.

# The Chronicles of Negroni

*THE CHRONICLES OF NARNIA* BY C. S. LEWIS

~~~~~~~~~~~~~~~~~~~~~~~~~~~~~~~~~~~~~~~~~

Since *The Chronicles of Narnia* were written out of chronological order, feel free to drink this one from any angle—right, left, upside down? We won't judge.

This is not your typical Negroni, not only because, well...the no-alcohol thing, but because this one has Edmund's sweet tooth in mind. You'll taste his courageous request for Turkish Delight in every sip—sans a run-in with the White Witch!

Although the books took Lewis over eight years to finish, this delightful recipe will take you under eight minutes to make.

~~~~~~~~~~~~~~~~~~~~~~~~~~~~~~~~~~~~~~~~~

## INGREDIENTS

1 oz rose water

1 oz red bitter soda

3 oz soda water

½ cup ice

1 edible rose for garnish

## INSTRUCTIONS

1. Fill a glass with ice.

2. Add in rose water, red bitter soda, and soda water.

3. Give it two to three gentle stirs.

4. Garnish the glass with an edible rose.

# The Adventures of Tom Collins

*THE ADVENTURES OF TOM SAWYER* BY MARK TWAIN

This refreshing lemon drink, with a splash of cranberry (a food Twain especially enjoyed), will clear your mind, cleanse your palate, and set the scene for your next adventure. It's the perfect escape from a long day. The best part? Traveling to an island to live out your days as a pirate is not required—you don't even have to leave your couch!

Just sit back, relax, and drink in the new beginnings.

## INGREDIENTS

3 pinches of sugar to coat rim

2 oz freshly squeezed lemon juice

½ cup cranberry juice

½ cup ice

⅓ cup soda water

Lemon or cherry for garnish

## INSTRUCTIONS

1. Wet your rim with a wedge of lemon and dip it in sugar.

2. In a shaker, combine lemon juice and cranberry juice. Shake well.

3. Fill a glass with ice and strain the shaker into the glass.

4. Top off with soda water, and gently stir.

5. Add the lemon or cherry as a garnish.

# Crime and Garnishment

*CRIME AND PUNISHMENT* BY FYODOR DOSTOEVSKY

~~~~~~~~~~~~~~~~~~~~~~~~~~~~~~~~~~~~~~~~~~~~~~~~~~

We're pairing one of the most popular drinks with one of Dostoevsky's most famous quotes, "And the more I drink the more I feel it. That's why I drink too. I try to find sympathy and feeling in drink... I drink so that I may suffer twice as much!"

So, this play on the gin and tonic has all the good feels—without the suffering.

Plus, as a nod to St. Petersburg, where the novel is set, we've added some delicious blueberries, since Russia is responsible for exporting nearly 90 percent of the world's blueberries.

~~~~~~~~~~~~~~~~~~~~~~~~~~~~~~~~~~~~~~~~~~~~~~~~~~

## INGREDIENTS

⅓ cup blueberries

2 Tbsp agave syrup

½ cup ice

¼ cup freshly squeezed lime juice

1 cup tonic water

1 lime wheel for garnish

*Or substitute blueberries and agave with 3 Tbsp berry simple syrup (see page 22)*

## INSTRUCTIONS

1. In a glass, combine blueberries and agave. Muddle until all of the blueberry juice is extracted.

2. Add in ice and lime juice. Give it a couple of stirs.

3. Top it off with tonic water, and gently stir once.

4. Garnish with a lime wheel, and drop in a few blueberries.

# The Invisible Manhattan

## THE INVISIBLE MAN BY H. G. WELLS AND INVISIBLE MAN BY RALPH ELLISON

This drink is inspired by two men—Jack Griffin from H. G. Wells's 1897 book *The Invisible Man*, and the unnamed narrator from Ralph Ellison's 1952 book *Invisible Man*. You'll notice that this beverage is quite the concoction, with way more ingredients than most others we've whipped up for you, but unlike Griffin's formula, the only thing this will make invisible is your thirst.

With much of Ellison's novel taking place in New York City, we felt it fitting that this be a dynamic take on a basic Manhattan.

## INGREDIENTS

½ cup ice

2 oz cranberry juice

2 oz apple juice

1 oz orange juice

1 Tbsp cherry juice

1 tsp lemon juice

1 dash of alcohol-free orange bitters

1 cherry for garnish

## INSTRUCTIONS

1. Chill your glass in the freezer for 30 minutes (ensure it's a freezer-safe glass).

2. In a shaker, combine cranberry juice, apple juice, orange juice, cherry juice, lemon juice, and orange bitters. Shake well for 30 seconds.

3. Fill your chilled glass with ice.

4. Strain the shaker into the glass. Give it a few stirs.

5. Garnish with a maraschino cherry.

# Moby-Sip

## *MOBY-DICK* BY HERMAN MELVILLE

We're honoring Mocha Dick, the real-life whale that inspired *Moby-Dick*—from which a character, Mr. Starbuck, inspired the name of an incredibly small coffeehouse chain.

Mocha Dick, who got his name from the island of Mocha in Chile—which he frequented, is a powerful star of nineteenth-century lore. And this drink will be the star of your mug during the chilly months.

Best paired with an ocean breeze while deeply respecting whales.

### INGREDIENTS

2 tsp cacao powder (or cocoa powder)

1 Tbsp agave syrup

1 cup vanilla almond milk

½ cup brewed coffee

Plant-based whipped cream for topping

Plant-based chocolate chips (or cacao nibs) for topping

### INSTRUCTIONS

1. Brew ½ cup of coffee—while your coffee is brewing, move on to step 2.

2. In a mug, add your cacao powder, agave, and almond milk. Give it a few stirs.

3. Add in your freshly brewed coffee, and stir until cacao powder and agave are dissolved.

4. Top off with plant-based whipped cream and chocolate chips.

# The 1984 French 75

## *1984* BY GEORGE ORWELL

Originally titled *The Last Man in Europe*, Orwell's *1984* is dripping with references to varieties of gin—each related to its respective social class. However, we've transformed this dystopian society into a utopian beverage. Gin-free, classism-free, and yum-ee.

Don't forget to garnish your drink with a lemon twist, or as we like to call it, the last twist in-your-cup...

### INGREDIENTS

2 cups ice

3 oz lemon juice

4 dashes alcohol-free orange bitters

12 oz tonic water

Lemon twist

Sugar for rim

### INSTRUCTIONS

1. In a mocktail shaker, combine ice, lemon juice, and bitters.

2. Shake until a bit icy, baby.

3. Sugar your rim and pour the shaker contents into a glass.

4. Top off with tonic water and give it a stir.

5. Garnish with a lemon twist.

# The Brave New World Old Fashioned

*BRAVE NEW WORLD* BY ALDOUS HUXLEY

Huxley hailed from Surrey, England, but moved to California in 1937, five years after *Brave New World* was published. The irony? Huxley wasn't a fan of what he considered to be California culture, and even attributed the themes of consumerism, delusion, and promiscuity depicted in *Brave New World* to a trip he'd taken to San Francisco in the '20s.

This drink is best enjoyed while soaking up the California sun, post-thrifting-spree.

## INGREDIENTS

2 tea bags of black tea

1 Tbsp freshly squeezed orange juice

2 dashes of alcohol-free aromatic bitters

1 tsp sugar

1 piece of orange peel

## INSTRUCTIONS

1. Boil 2 cups of water and steep the black tea for 5 minutes. Refrigerate for 20 minutes to cool.

2. In a glass, combine 1 Tbsp freshly squeezed orange juice, bitters, and sugar.

3. Give it a good few stirs and drop in a fancy ice cube.

4. Pour in your brewed black tea and stir until chilled.

5. Coat your rim with the inside of a piece of orange peel and drop it into the glass.

# Banned Books

Unlike your favorite banned book, these drinks are not off-limits.
In fact, we encourage seconds.

# The Grape Gatsby

*THE GREAT GATSBY* BY F. SCOTT FITZGERALD

Some deliciously sweet, others deceptively sour, you could say grapes are the characters of Fitzgerald's *The Great Gatsby* personified. Climbing the tendrils of society, Gatsby and his guests may appear smooth-skinned and beautiful, but who knows what truly lurks beneath? Will you choose to sprinkle some edible gold on this drink for a sophisticated twist? Or will you keep it classic, knowing that not all that glitters is gold?

## INGREDIENTS

**1 cup seedless grapes (red or green), halved**

**4–6 fresh basil leaves**

**½ oz fresh lime juice**

**½ oz simple syrup (see page 20)**

**Soda water or soda water**

**Ice cubes**

**Basil leaves and grape skewer for garnish**

**Edible gold, for a Gatsby twist**

## INSTRUCTIONS

1. In a cocktail shaker or sturdy glass, muddle the seedless grapes and fresh basil leaves together until well mashed and fragrant.

2. Add fresh lime juice and simple syrup to the muddled grapes and basil.

3. Fill the shaker or glass with ice cubes.

4. Shake or stir well to combine all the ingredients.

5. Strain the mixture into a glass filled with fresh ice cubes.

6. Top up the glass with soda water. Gently stir.

7. Garnish with basil and a skewer of grapes. If you are feeling so Gatsby, sprinkle in some edible gold.

# Are You There Goblet? It's Me, Margaret.

*ARE YOU THERE GOD? IT'S ME, MARGARET.* BY JUDY BLUME

We must, we must, we must increase our...trust. When it comes to getting to know yourself without booze, remember that it is a journey. Just as Margaret is figuring out her own relationship with God, her body, and her new school, you too can figure out life without booze. Feel your feelings and remember to give yourself grace.

This version of a Midori Splice is sweet and tart, perfect for balancing all the feelings life throws at you, no matter what age you are.

## INGREDIENTS

1½ oz melon flavored syrup

2 oz coconut cream

2 oz pineapple juice

1 oz fresh lime juice

1 oz agave syrup (adjust to taste)

Ice cubes

Pineapple wedge and maraschino cherry for garnish

## INSTRUCTIONS

1. In a shaker, combine melon flavored syrup, coconut cream, pineapple juice, lime juice, and agave syrup.

2. Add a handful of ice cubes to the shaker.

3. Shake well until the mixture is thoroughly chilled.

4. Strain the mixture into a glass filled with ice cubes.

5. Garnish with a pineapple wedge and a maraschino cherry, and enjoy!

# Stone Berry Blue Lagoon

## *STONE BUTCH BLUES* BY LESLIE FEINBERG

If one word could describe both Leslie Feinberg's *Stone Butch Blues* and this drink, *"vibrant"* would cover every grain of sand on the beach. Served over ice in a highball glass, the visually appealing Stone Berry Blue Lagoon has a literal cherry on top to make any hot summer day just perfect.

## INGREDIENTS

1 oz blue curaçao syrup or blue raspberry syrup

1 oz fresh lime juice

2 oz lemon-lime soda

Ice cubes

Orange slice or twist for garnish (optional)

## INSTRUCTIONS

1. Fill a glass with ice cubes.

2. Pour the blue curaçao syrup or blue raspberry syrup over the ice.

3. Add fresh lime juice to the glass.

4. Top up the glass with lemon-lime soda.

5. Stir gently to mix the ingredients and chill the drink.

6. Garnish with an orange slice or twist if desired.

# Frankenstein's Fuzzy Navel

*FRANKENSTEIN* BY MARY SHELLEY

Unstoppable. Devilish. Sociable. These are a few of the words used to describe Frankenstein's monster. It's not a far reach to say they also describe this satisfyingly sippable libation. No lab coat or beakers needed.

## INGREDIENTS

3 oz orange juice

3 oz peach nectar or peach juice

½ oz fresh lemon juice

Ice cubes

Peach slice for garnish

Optional: simple syrup (see page 20) or agave syrup

## INSTRUCTIONS

1. Fill a glass with ice cubes.

2. Pour the orange juice into the glass.

3. Add the peach nectar or peach juice to the glass.

4. Squeeze in fresh lemon juice.

5. If using, pour in the simple syrup or agave syrup for added sweetness (adjust to taste).

6. Stir gently to mix the ingredients.

7. Garnish with a peach slice if desired.

# Alice's Adventures in Soberland

*ALICE'S ADVENTURES IN WONDERLAND* BY LEWIS CARROLL

Life is often stranger than fiction. And sober life can prove to be so intoxicating that an entire Soberland visited by Alice is filled with delicious excitement. You don't have to be "mad" to come to this tea party. Hats off to you if you drink it—we promise it won't make you shrink.

## INGREDIENTS

½ cup brewed berry-infused tea

¼ cup lemonade

2 Tbsp orange juice

1 Tbsp agave

Sliced citrus fruits and/or mint leaves for garnish

## INSTRUCTIONS

1. Brew the fruit-infused tea according to the package instructions and allow it to cool to room temperature.

2. In a glass or small pitcher, combine the brewed tea, lemonade, orange juice, and agave. Stir until the agave is fully dissolved.

3. Add ice cubes to the glass or pitcher to chill the mocktail.

4. Slice citrus fruits (lemons, oranges, and/or limes) and add them to the glass as a decorative garnish.

# The Blizzard of Oz

*THE WONDERFUL WIZARD OF OZ* BY L. FRANK BAUM

~~~~~~~~~~~~~~~~~~~~~~~~~~~~~~~~~~~~~~~~~~~~~~~~~~~~~~~~~

Swirled around and flipped upside down, Dorothy's tornado turned her life into vibrantly colored sprinkles. Animal cracker lions and tigers and bears (oh my!) add a crunch to this blizzard that promises not to bite back. Follow the yellow brick road and enjoy. Just be sure to make enough to share with the entire Lollipop Guild.

~~~~~~~~~~~~~~~~~~~~~~~~~~~~~~~~~~~~~~~~~~~~~~~~~~~~~~~~~

## INGREDIENTS

1 cup unsweetened almond milk (or any plant-based milk of your choice)

1 cup plant-based vanilla ice cream

¼ cup animal crackers (plus extra for garnish)

1 tsp agave syrup

Sprinkles

## INSTRUCTIONS

1. In a blender, combine the almond milk, vanilla ice cream, and animal crackers. Blend until smooth.

2. Prepare the glass: Crush animal crackers and mix with sprinkles. Add agave syrup to a plate. Dip cocktail glass into the syrup, then dip the rimmed glass into the crushed animal crackers and sprinkles mixture.

3. Pour into the prepared glass.

4. Garnish with whole plant-based animal crackers and extra sprinkles.

**Note:** If you are feeling extra fancy, you can use a plant-based food dye and layer the shake with the colors of the rainbow.

# Catcher in the Mai Tai

## THE CATCHER IN THE RYE BY J. D. SALINGER

Just like Holden Caulfield, the Mai Tai is layered and complex. Sweet, tart, and nutty, one would think this mix of flavors would cause confusion, but they come together in a perfect blend that will please generations past and present…and many more to come.

### INGREDIENTS

2 oz pineapple juice

1 oz orange juice

½ oz lime juice

½ oz orgeat syrup (almond syrup)

½ oz grenadine syrup

½ oz soda water or soda water

Ice cubes

Pineapple slice, cherry, and mint sprig for garnish

### INSTRUCTIONS

1. Fill a shaker or mixing glass with ice cubes.

2. Add the pineapple juice, orange juice, lime juice, orgeat syrup, and grenadine syrup to the shaker.

3. Shake well until the mixture is thoroughly chilled.

4. Strain the mixture into a glass filled with ice cubes.

5. Top up the glass with soda water or soda water.

6. Stir gently to mix.

7. Garnish with a pineapple slice, cherry, and mint sprig.

# The Well (Drink) of Loneliness

*THE WELL OF LONELINESS* BY RADCLYFFE HALL

A nod to Radclyffe Hall's *The Well of Loneliness*, a novel that explores the multifaceted main character and her journey to find acceptance in society. Accepting what may seem unconventional and, in fact, outright controversial can prove to be a delight—just like the ingredients of this libation.

## INGREDIENTS

½ cup brewed black tea

½ tsp maple syrup or molasses

¼ tsp vanilla extract

¼ tsp almond extract

1 Tbsp fresh lime juice

1 can (12 oz) cola

Ice cubes

Lime wedge and fresh mint for garnish

## INSTRUCTIONS

1. Brew a strong black tea and let it cool completely. This will serve as the base to mimic the depth and complexity of rum.

2. In a shaker or mixing glass, combine the cooled black tea, molasses or maple syrup, vanilla extract, almond extract, and fresh lime juice. Stir well until the molasses or maple syrup is fully dissolved and all ingredients are well combined.

3. Fill a tall glass with ice cubes.

4. Pour the tea mixture over the ice and top up with cola, gently stirring to combine.

5. Garnish with a lime wedge and a sprig of fresh mint for a refreshing touch.

# Huckleberry Fizz

*ADVENTURES OF HUCKLEBERRY FINN* BY MARK TWAIN

The first edition of *Huckleberry Finn* had a slight issue as the book went to press. Someone had interfered with one of the illustrations by adding a "bulge" to the pants of Uncle Silas in a scene where he talked with Aunt Sally and Huck. This could have been a disaster for Twain, but luckily it was caught and corrected early enough. To this day, nobody knows who did it.

We're reinventing the concept of a "stiff drink" with this adventure in a glass.

## INGREDIENTS

5 huckleberries

1 Tbsp lime juice

4 mint leaves

1 tsp agave syrup

1 cup blackberry kombucha

Lime wheel

## INSTRUCTIONS

1. In a glass, muddle the huckleberries, lime, and agave.

2. Grab your mint in one hand, spank your mint with the other hand to release its oils, and drop it into the glass.

3. Add in your kombucha and give it a stir.

4. Garnish with a lime wheel.

# Strong Quixote

## *DON QUIXOTE* BY MIGUEL DE CERVANTES

We have Cervantes to thank for popularizing the phrase, "The proof is in the pudding." However, that's not exactly what he wrote. The original phrase, "the proof of the pudding is in the eating," was translated to English in 1701 as, "the proof is in the pudding." Either way, it sounds delicious.

This banana cream pudding-inspired libation is best served with delusions of grandeur. It's idealism in a glass!

### INGREDIENTS

2 tsp plant-based caramel sauce

4 plant-based vanilla wafers, to crush for rim

1 overripe banana

2 cups almond milk

1 cup plant-based vanilla yogurt

½ banana, to slice for garnish

Plant-based whipped cream for topping

### INSTRUCTIONS

1. Dip the rim of your glass in the caramel sauce, and then in the crushed vanilla wafers.

2. In a blender, combine banana, almond milk, and yogurt. Blend until smooth and creamy.

3. Pour this sweet, creamy goodness into a glass.

4. Add some sliced banana and whipped cream for garnish.

# The Sundae Also Rises

## *THE SUN ALSO RISES* BY ERNEST HEMINGWAY

In the spirit of Hemingway's minimalist approach to writing, you'll only need a short list of simple ingredients for this mocktail. Less is more for these strong flavors to shine, much as the minimal dialogue in *The Sun Also Rises* enables the characters' inner experience to take center stage.

Enjoy this nod to Hemingway's favorite drink—the strawberry daiquiri—and extra cool if you can use wild strawberries, as mentioned in the novel.

## INGREDIENTS

2 cups frozen strawberries

⅓ cup fresh lime juice

1 cup ice

1 cup tonic water

1 scoop plant-based coconut ice cream and sliced strawberry for garnish

## INSTRUCTIONS

1. Chill your glass in the freezer for 30 minutes (ensure it's a freezer safe glass).

2. In a blender, combine strawberries, lime juice, and ice. Blend until smooth.

3. Pour into chilled glass, add in desired amount of tonic water, and give it one or two stirs.

4. Add a scoop of ice cream and a sliced strawberry for garnish.

# The Oliver Lemon Twist

## OLIVER TWIST BY CHARLES DICKENS

This refreshment awakens the senses, like the fresh perspective Oliver Twist gave the public on the reality of workhouses. The lime represents the bitterness of injustice, simple syrup the sweetness of hope, and the soda water embodies Oliver's sparkling spirit.

And yes, you can have more.

### INGREDIENTS

2 pinches of sugar to coat the rim

3 ice cubes

2 Tbsp lemon juice

1 Tbsp simple syrup (see page 20)

1 cup soda water

Lemon twist for garnish

### INSTRUCTIONS

1.  Wet the rim of your glass with a lemon wedge and dip it in sugar.

2.  In a shaker, combine a few ice cubes, lemon juice, and simple syrup. Shake until chilled.

3.  Strain into your glass and top it off with soda water.

4.  Garnish with a lemon twist.

# A Clockwork Orange Crush

### *A CLOCKWORK ORANGE* BY ANTHONY BURGESS

If "goodness is something chosen," we've chosen this—and it's damn good.

The next time you want to discuss a nice, light topic like the nature of humanity, feel free to pair that chat with this creamy treat. Unlike the spiked milk in *A Clockwork Orange*, this milky mocktail is not only safe for consumption, but absolutely delicious.

## INGREDIENTS

1 cup ice

1 cup freshly squeezed orange juice

⅓ cup plant-based vanilla creamer

¼ cup soda water

Plant-based whipped cream for garnish

Orange wheel for garnish

## INSTRUCTIONS

1. Fill a glass with ice.

2. Pour the orange juice and vanilla creamer over the ice and give it a stir.

3. Add in your soda water and stir one or two times.

4. Top off with your desired amount of whipped cream (don't be shy) and an orange wheel for garnish.

# James and the Giant Peach Bellini

*JAMES AND THE GIANT PEACH* BY ROALD DAHL

Did you know *James and the Giant Peach* was almost *James and the Giant Cherry*?

Dahl's apple orchard influenced this work, and he considered several fruits for the story that just didn't feel right before he landed on the "prettier, bigger, and squishier" peach.

This being his first children's book, he wanted to incorporate animal characters, but felt everyone had already written about them. "Little things" like insects, however, nobody seemed to have explored yet. A good reminder not to forget the little guys!

Dahl dedicated this book to his daughter, and we've dedicated this beverage to you.

## INGREDIENTS

½ cup chilled plant-based peach nectar (or peach juice)

½ chilled soda water

Sliced peaches for garnish

## INSTRUCTIONS

1. Chill your glass in the freezer for 30 minutes (ensure it's a freezer-safe glass).

2. Pour in your peach nectar, then your soda water. Give it a stir.

3. Add a slice of peach to your rim, or inside your glass, for garnish.

# Of Mice and Menthol

## *OF MICE AND MEN* BY JOHN STEINBECK

~~~~~~~~~~~~~~~~~~~~~~~~~~~~~~~~~~~~~~~~~~~~~~~~~~~~~~~~~~~~~~~~~~~

Originally titled *Something that Happened,* this book was something that almost didn't happen, due to something that actually happened that sounds like an absurd, childish lie. Steinbeck's dog, Max, ate the first draft.

So, this thirst-quencher has mint in it, which is toxic to dogs. Your dog can't eat it, which will help you avoid ruined days and career setbacks. You're welcome.

~~~~~~~~~~~~~~~~~~~~~~~~~~~~~~~~~~~~~~~~~~~~~~~~~~~~~~~~~~~~~~~~~~~

### INGREDIENTS

1½ cups nonalcoholic ginger beer (or ginger ale)

⅓ cup mint simple syrup

1 cup crushed ice

1 sprig of mint for garnish

### INSTRUCTIONS

1. Fill your glass with crushed ice.

2. Pour in the ginger beer.

3. Add in the mint syrup, and give it one or two stirs.

4. Garnish with a sprig of mint.

# Book-to-Movie

# Adaptations

Was the book or the movie better? Luckily with these drinks,
you won't have to decide.

# Soda & Sensibility

*SENSE AND SENSIBILITY* BY JANE AUSTEN

This drink combines Elinor's romantic sense (cranberry, orange, and lemon) with Marianne's medicinal sensibility (agave and mint). This combination of tart flavors with the final sweetness of the agave syrup provides the perfect balance of reason and passion.

Top with soda water to give it an extra fizz, which makes it perfect for an afternoon of leisurely reading your favorite Jane Austen novel.

## INGREDIENTS

1 oz cranberry juice

1 oz orange juice

1 oz lemon juice

1 tsp agave syrup

Fresh mint leaves

Soda water

Ice cubes

Orange slice (for garnish)

Fresh mint leaves (for garnish)

## INSTRUCTIONS

1. In a cocktail shaker, combine cranberry juice, orange juice, lemon juice, agave, and fresh mint.

2. Shake well to mix the ingredients until the agave is dissolved.

3. Fill a glass with ice cubes.

4. Strain the juice mixture over the ice cubes in the glass.

5. Top it off with soda water and gently stir.

6. Garnish the glass with an orange slice and fresh mint leaves.

# Gone with the Wine

*GONE WITH THE WIND* BY MARGARET MITCHELL

~~~~~~~~~~~~~~~~~~~~~~~~~~~~~~~~~~~~~~~~~~~~~~~~~~~~~~~~~~~~~~~~

Just as Scarlett O'Hara comes into her own in Margaret Mitchell's *Gone with the Wind*, so do the dried hibiscus flowers in this uncommon and refreshing take on wine. Infused with grape juice, agave syrup, and fresh lemon, serve this over ice for a transformation fit for a Southern belle.

~~~~~~~~~~~~~~~~~~~~~~~~~~~~~~~~~~~~~~~~~~~~~~~~~~~~~~~~~~~~~~~~

## INGREDIENTS

¼ cup dried hibiscus flowers

1 cup hot water

½ cup grape juice

¼ cup simple syrup (see page 20) or agave syrup (adjust to taste)

½ oz fresh lemon juice

Ice cubes

Fresh grapes for garnish

Lemon slice for garnish

## INSTRUCTIONS

1. In a heatproof container, combine the dried hibiscus flowers and hot water.

2. Let the hibiscus steep in the hot water for about 10–15 minutes to make hibiscus tea. Strain and discard the flowers, then allow the tea to cool to room temperature.

3. In a pitcher or mixing glass, combine the hibiscus tea, grape juice, simple syrup or agave syrup, and fresh lemon juice.

4. Stir well to mix the ingredients.

5. Fill the glass with ice cubes.

6. Pour the mixture into the glass.

7. Garnish with fresh grapes and a lemon slice.

**Note:** Makes four glasses. Refrigerate immediately.

# Zero-Proof Expectations

## *GREAT EXPECTATIONS* BY CHARLES DICKENS

Expectations can be funny things. You may not expect an orphaned boy to become suddenly wealthy via an unknown benefactor, but this is exactly what happens to Pip. The *Great Expectations* protagonist is just as complex as the mincemeat pie he stole—the very one that inspired this drink. And you may expect a mincemeat-inspired beverage to contain, well, meat. But what did we say again about expectations being funny things?

## INGREDIENTS

2 cups apple juice

½ cup raisins

¼ cup currants

¼ cup candied citron peel

Peel of 1 lemon

Peel of 1 orange

¼ tsp ground nutmeg

1 apple, thinly sliced

Ice cubes

Soda water

Lemon or orange slices for garnish

## INSTRUCTIONS

1. In a saucepan, combine the apple juice, raisins, currants, candied citron peel, lemon peel, orange peel, ground nutmeg, and sliced apple. Heat on low, stirring occasionally, for about 10–15 minutes. Be careful not to boil.

2. Remove the saucepan from heat and let the mixture cool completely.

3. Once cooled, strain the mixture into a pitcher to remove the fruit peels and solids. Chill for at least 1 hour.

4. Fill a glass with ice, pour the chilled fruit-infused juice into the glasses, filling each about halfway. Top with soda water.

5. Garnish each glass with a slice of lemon or orange.

# Little Women, Big Gimlet

## *LITTLE WOMEN* BY LOUISA MAY ALCOTT

While many things changed over the years for Meg, Jo, Beth, and Amy, lemonade remained a constant in the March household. From childhood to adulthood, this refreshing drink is fit for any season or phase of life.

### INGREDIENTS

**2 oz lemon juice (freshly squeezed if possible)**

**½ oz lavender syrup (see page 21)**

**3 oz tonic water or soda water**

**Ice cubes**

**Lemon wedge and lavender sprig for garnish**

### INSTRUCTIONS

1. Fill a glass with ice cubes.

2. Pour the lemon juice into the glass.

3. Add the lavender syrup.

4. Stir gently to mix.

5. Top up the glass with tonic water or soda water.

6. Stir again to combine.

7. Garnish with a lime wedge and lavender sprig.

# Jane Love is in the Eyre Martini

*JANE EYRE* BY CHARLOTTE BRONTE

While Jane Eyre's life was full of trials and tribulations, forcing her to emerge as a resilient heroine, not everything in life has to be so hard. Sometimes, you just get to have some cake. This elixir boasts inviting tea-cake-inspired flavors of vanilla and almond that will definitely have you asking for a spot more.

## INGREDIENTS

½ cup brewed vanilla rooibos tea, chilled

¼ cup plant-based milk

1 Tbsp vanilla syrup or simple syrup (see page 20 or 22)

¼ tsp almond extract

Ice cubes

Ground cinnamon or nutmeg for garnish

## INSTRUCTIONS

1. Brew vanilla rooibos tea and let it cool completely in the refrigerator.

2. In a shaker or mixing glass, combine the chilled vanilla rooibos tea, milk, vanilla syrup or simple syrup, and almond extract.

3. Fill the shaker with ice cubes.

4. Shake well until the mixture is thoroughly chilled.

5. Strain the mixture into a martini glass.

6. Garnish with a sprinkle of ground cinnamon or nutmeg.

# The Color Purple Cos-No

## *THE COLOR PURPLE* BY ALICE WALKER

If one were going to write home (or to God) about a mocktail, it would be this one. The perfect blend of berry juices, lime, and agave syrup offers delight for both the eyes and the tongue.

### INGREDIENTS

2 oz cranberry juice

1 oz blueberry juice or blueberry syrup (see page 22)

½ oz fresh lime juice

½ oz simple syrup (see page 20) or agave syrup

Ice cubes

Blueberry skewer for garnish

### INSTRUCTIONS

1. Fill a shaker or mixing glass with ice cubes.

2. Add the cranberry juice, blueberry juice (or blueberry syrup), fresh lime juice, and simple syrup (or agave syrup) to the shaker.

3. Shake well until the mixture is thoroughly chilled.

4. Strain the mixture into a chilled glass filled with ice cubes.

5. Garnish with a skewer of blueberries.

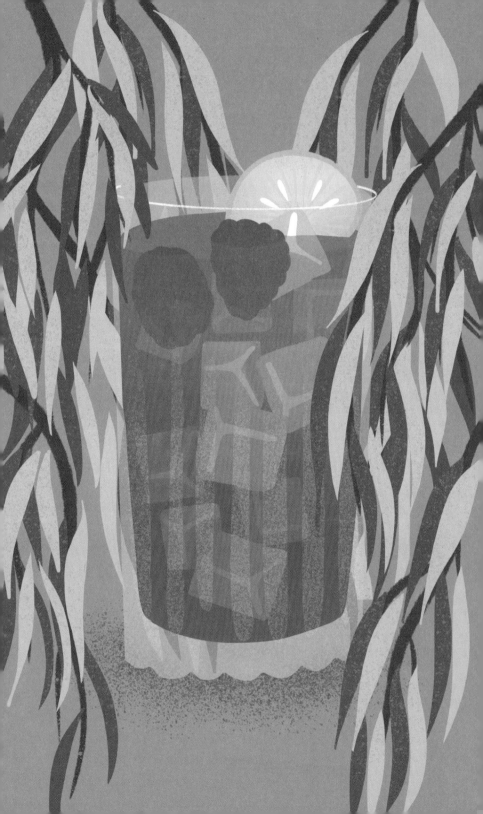

# Beloved Bramble

### *BELOVED* BY TONI MORRISON

A bramble can be both prickly and sweet (much like life). This is a nod to Toni Morrison and her unrelenting dedication to shining a spotlight on the human psyche and the resilience of the human spirit. Pair this with your favorite Southern biscuit—perhaps like those Sethe prepares for Paul in *Beloved*.

## INGREDIENTS

**2 oz blackberry juice or blackberry syrup (see page 22)**

**1 oz fresh lemon juice**

**½ oz simple syrup (see page 20) or agave syrup (optional)**

**Soda water or soda water**

**Ice cubes**

**Fresh blackberries and lemon slice for garnish**

## INSTRUCTIONS

1. Fill a glass with ice cubes.

2. Pour the blackberry juice or blackberry syrup into the glass.

3. Add fresh lemon juice to the glass.

4. If using, pour in the simple syrup or agave syrup for added sweetness.

5. Stir gently to mix the ingredients.

6. Top up the glass with soda water or soda water.

7. Stir again to combine.

8. Garnish with fresh blackberries and a lemon slice.

# The Horchata on Mango Street

*THE HOUSE ON MANGO STREET* BY SANDRA CISNEROS

Chicago's summer heat ignites a thirst that can be quenched by this mango-sweetened horchata. Notes of vanilla and cinnamon marry deliciously in a way that would make any abuela say *"Sabroso!"*

## INGREDIENTS

1 ripe mango, peeled and diced (or 1 cup of frozen mango chunks)

1 cup cooked rice

4 cups water

½ cup granulated sugar (adjust to taste)

1 tsp ground cinnamon

1 tsp vanilla extract

Ice cubes

Mango slices and mint leaves for garnish

## INSTRUCTIONS

1. In a blender, combine the diced mango, cooked rice, water, granulated sugar, ground cinnamon, and vanilla extract.

2. Blend on high speed until the mixture is smooth and well combined.

3. Strain the mixture through a fine mesh sieve or cheesecloth into a pitcher to remove any bits.

4. Refrigerate the horchata mixture for at least 1–2 hours, or until chilled.

5. Once chilled, fill glasses with ice cubes and pour the mixture into them.

6. Garnish with mango slices or mint leaves if desired.

**Note:** Serves four.

# Les Minterables

*LES MISÉRABLES* BY VICTOR HUGO

As the face of *Les Misérables* and the anchor of the story, the character of Cosette symbolizes hope and resilience—although her spirit could've easily been hardened by the loss and injustice she experienced.

We're channeling Cosette's journey, and essence, into this shake with the beloved flavor of mint chocolate—with the chocolate chips representing the hardships and hurdles, amidst the lightness of mint, which envelops your tastebuds.

It's a castle on a cloud in a cup.

## INGREDIENTS

2 scoops plant-based mint chip ice cream

2 cups almond milk

1 cup ice

1 sprig of mint for garnish

## INSTRUCTIONS

1. In a blender, combine ice cream, almond milk, and ice.

2. Blend until smooth.

3. Top off with a sprig of mint for garnish.

# Flight Club

## *FIGHT CLUB* BY CHUCK PALAHNIUK

Let's talk about the real star of *Fight Club*, the soap.

This little bar really packs a punch (pun intended) by representing all the main themes—anti-consumerism, violence, rebellion, transformation, the hypocrisy of modern society, and the satirical commentary on masculinity and femininity.

Playing off the latter, in this flight you'll find elegant and flowery flavors and (soapy?) aromas that delight the senses, amidst...a stereotypical beery dude drink.

### INGREDIENTS

½ cup brewed chamomile tea

½ cup brewed rose tea

½ cup brewed lavender tea

½ cups nonalcoholic ginger beer

1 edible chamomile for garnish

1 edible rose for garnish

1 edible lavender for garnish

### INSTRUCTIONS

1. Bring 2 cups of water to a boil. In 3 glasses, steep chamomile tea, rose tea, and lavender tea separately for 5 minutes.

2. Let the teas cool and refrigerate for 20 minutes.

3. Add your ginger beer to each brewed tea.

4. Top off with your edible chamomile, rose, and lavender in each respective glass for garnish.

# There Will Be Bloody Mary

## *OIL!* BY UPTON SINCLAIR

Although the novel, *Oil!*, and the film loosely based on it, *There Will Be Blood*, have many differences, the one thing they have in common is showcasing the fiery destruction greed wreaks on the human soul.

Not dissimilar to the burning oil rig in both works, this delicious, smoky "tower of flame" is "the most amazing spectacle" as it's stacked with a variety of crowd-pleasing garnishes. This Sunday brunch favorite will leave admirers asking themselves, "Why don't I own this?"

### INGREDIENTS

1 lemon wedge

2 Tbsp celery salt

½ cup of ice

1 cup tomato juice

2 Tbsp freshly squeezed lemon juice

1 Tbsp soy sauce (or plant-based Worcestershire sauce)

1 pinch of black pepper

Garnish: 1 celery stalk

### INSTRUCTIONS

1. Wet the rim of your glass using a lemon wedge and dip it in celery salt.

2. In a glass, combine ice, tomato juice, lemon juice, soy sauce, and black pepper.

3. Give it a few gentle stirs.

4. Garnish with celery stalk.

**Want to indulge?** Stack your garnish stick with 1 pickle, 3 green olives, 1 lime wedge, and ¼ plant-based meat patty.

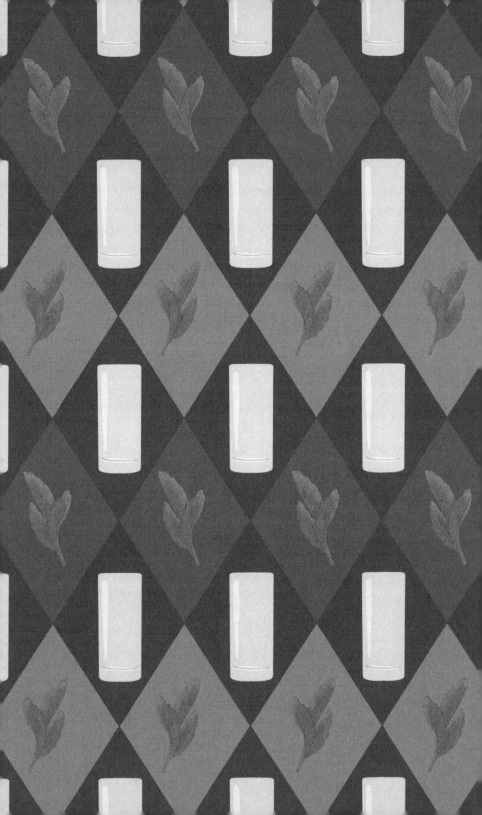

# The Devil Drinks Wada

*THE DEVIL WEARS PRADA* BY LAUREN WEISBERGER

~~~~~~~~~~~~~~~~~~~~~~~~~~~~~~~~~~~~~~~~~~~~~~~~~~~~~~~~~~~~~~~~

This drink is dedicated to legendary diva, Miranda Priestly.

First, experience the bite of tangy lime that rattles your tastebuds, the way Miranda's sharp-tongued one-liners pierce Andy's very soul, then a burst of sparkling water for all of the bubbly assistants whose dreams were crushed in her presence. Moving on to the fresh mint, like Miranda's pristine sense of style, followed by the sweetness of agave, which—like her back-handed compliments—leaves you wanting more. Finally, the frosty ice that lingers on your lips, just like her icy stare that sends shivers down your spine.

Feel free to drink this "at a glacial pace."

~~~~~~~~~~~~~~~~~~~~~~~~~~~~~~~~~~~~~~~~~~~~~~~~~~~~~~~~~~~~~~~~

## INGREDIENTS

8 mint leaves

2 oz agave

3 oz fresh lime juice

½ cup soda water

⅓ cup ice

For garnish: 1 lime wheel, 1 sprig of mint

## INSTRUCTIONS

1. In a shaker, throw your mint leaves in and muddle them a bit.

2. Add your agave and lime juice and shake until the agave is dissolved.

3. Fill your glass with ice, and strain the contents of your shaker over the ice.

4. Top off with soda water.

5. Add your lime wheel to the rim, and drop your sprig of mint in for garnish.

# The Talented Mr. Sipley

## *THE TALENTED MR. RIPLEY* BY PATRICIA HIGHSMITH

Inspired by Tom Ripley's international adventures, this Italian-inspired hot chocolate is just as thick as his web of lies. This warm, sweet, simple luxury is the perfect complement to Tom's cold, callous behavior as he pursues extravagance, wealth, and influence at all costs.

This decadent drink will surely become your new obsession. Enjoy anywhere—except on a boat with Mr. Ripley.

### INGREDIENTS

**4 oz plant-based chocolate chips**

**2 Tbsp cocoa powder**

**1 Tbsp sugar**

**2 cups almond milk**

**3 tsp cornstarch**

**1 pinch of salt**

**Plant-based marshmallows for garnish**

### INSTRUCTIONS

1. In a saucepan, add chocolate chips, cocoa powder, and sugar.

2. Heat and stir until melted.

3. Add in the milk, cornstarch, and salt. Stir until smooth.

4. Pour into your mug.

5. Top off with marshmallows for garnish.

# The Joy Luck Club Soda

## *THE JOY LUCK CLUB* BY AMY TAN

Food provides powerful symbolism in Amy Tan's novel, or what she describes as a collection of short stories that she never intended to make up a book.

The food in *The Joy Luck Club* is used to show both connection and division, throughout the variety of experiences these mothers and daughters navigate together.

For this recipe, we're combining two key flavors mentioned in the book—the gift of salted plums from Waverley's mom and of course oranges (for good luck)!

### INGREDIENTS

1 cup ice

⅓ cup plum juice

⅓ cup freshly squeezed orange juice

⅓ cup soda water

1 plum wedge for garnish

### INSTRUCTIONS

1. In a shaker, add a few ice cubes, plum juice, and orange juice.

2. Shake well for 30 seconds.

3. Fill glass with ice.

4. Strain the shaker over the ice.

5. Top off with soda water. Stir gently one or two times.

6. Add a plum wedge to the rim for garnish.

# Their Ryes Were Watching God

*THEIR EYES WERE WATCHING GOD* BY ZORA NEALE HURSTON

Our eyes were watching Janie Mae Crawford, and this recipe is all about her.

This sweet, earthy drink with a dash of cinnamon is as grounding as Janie's confidence and independence, spicy like her desire for true love and fulfillment, and comforting like her favorite pear tree that taught her endless lessons about life.

Best enjoyed under "any tree in bloom!"

## INGREDIENTS

½ cup barley tea

½ cup of ice

½ cup pear juice

1 pinch of cinnamon

1 cinnamon stick for garnish

## INSTRUCTIONS

1. Brew 1 cup of barley tea, and let cool for 20 minutes.

2. Fill a glass with ice.

3. Pour in the pear juice, then the barley tea, followed by the pinch of cinnamon.

4. Give it five stirs.

5. Garnish with a stick of cinnamon.

# Book Clubs

Drinks to make for your next book club or gathering.
Come for the banter, stay for the beverages.

# The Sober Garden

## *THE SECRET GARDEN* BY FRANCES HODGSON BURNETT

Ever stumble across something that offers surprise after surprise in the best way possible? Just as Mary Lennox transformed a hidden and neglected garden into something glorious, this drink takes fruit, flowers, fizz, and fun flavors and turns them into a beverage that is nothing short of magical. Cheers to finding amazement in unexpected places.

### INGREDIENTS

6 cups water

¼ cup dried hibiscus flowers

1 cup mixed berries (such as strawberries, raspberries, and blueberries)

½ cup fresh lemon juice

½ cup simple syrup (see page 20) (adjust to taste)

1 liter soda water

Ice cubes

Edible flowers for garnish

### INSTRUCTIONS

1. In a large saucepan, bring the water to a boil.

2. Remove from heat and add the dried hibiscus flowers. Let steep for 10–15 minutes.

3. Strain and discard the flowers, then cool to room temperature.

4. In a large punch bowl or pitcher, combine the hibiscus tea, mixed berries, fresh lemon juice, and simple syrup.

5. Refrigerate the punch mixture for at least 1–2 hours, or until chilled.

6. Once chilled, add the soda water to the punch mixture and stir gently to combine.

7. Serve over ice and garnish with edible flowers.

# Sober-lastic Book Fair

There's something for everyone at the Sober-lastic Book Fair! And just like the book fairs of days gone by, the perfect-for-you treasure is exactly what you'll find at the DIY beverage bar. Edible glitter, flowers, and a rainbow of syrups and juices will pair perfectly with your bubblegum, erasers, unicorn notes, and dinosaur posters. The more the merrier, so be sure to invite your friends.

## INGREDIENTS

Plain soda water

Ice

Ice bucket

Various syrups (lavender, blue curaçao syrup) (see pages 20–22)

Various juices (orange, cranberry, grape)

Edible glitter

Edible flowers

Assorted glassware

## INSTRUCTIONS

1. To set up the Sober-lastic Book Fair, display the ingredients so guests can make their own desired mocktail.

# Rubyfruit Jungle Juice

## *RUBYFRUIT JUNGLE* BY RITA MAE BROWN

A "traditional" Jungle Juice is often the first foray forging a formative path to other drinks—its improvisation being one of intrigue and ease. The Rubyfruit Jungle Juice raises the bar on the timeless classic by offering a diverse mix of flavors that are an ode to authenticity and independence: no alcohol required, no hangover expected.

### INGREDIENTS

4 cups pineapple juice

2 cups orange juice

2 cups cranberry juice

2 cups lemon-lime soda or ginger ale

¼ cup grenadine syrup

Assorted fresh fruit slices (such as oranges, pineapples, strawberries, and kiwis) for garnish

Ice cubes

### INSTRUCTIONS

1. In a large punch bowl or pitcher, combine the pineapple juice, orange juice, and cranberry juice.

2. Add the lemon-lime soda or ginger ale to the juice mixture and stir gently to combine.

3. Slowly pour in the grenadine syrup, allowing it to sink to the bottom of the bowl or pitcher.

4. Add ice cubes to chill the mixture.

5. Garnish with assorted fresh fruit slices and stir before serving.

6. Serve in individual glasses filled with ice cubes.

# The Shotfather

*THE GODFATHER* BY MARIO PUZO

We've made you a drink you can't refuse.

The drinks are plentiful and prevalent in *The Godfather*. Scotch is flowin' during business meetings, red wine makes its rounds at family dinners and events, and white wine is the go-to for parties.

However, we're drawing inspiration from amaretto—a drink Don Corleone enjoys sipping at his desk at, well, any time.

Feel free to serve this to the family, at dinner parties, or even to your co-workers during work hours.

## INGREDIENTS

6 cups water

2½ cups brown sugar

5 Tbsp almond extract

5 tsp vanilla extract

## INSTRUCTIONS

1. In a saucepan, bring the water and sugar to a boil.

2. Reduce the heat until sugar is dissolved. Stir occasionally.

3. Remove from heat and let cool for 30 minutes.

4. Add the almond and vanilla extract to the saucepan. Stir six times.

5. Pour into a shot glass and enjoy at room temperature.

**Note:** Makes about five shots.

# Ceremony Caipirinha

## *CEREMONY* BY LESLIE MARMON SILKO

~~~~~~~~~~~~~~~~~~~~~~~~~~~~~~~~~~~~~~~~~~~~~~~~~~~

Tayo's transformation encompasses a deepening connection to nature, a respect for culture and tradition, and ultimately the acceptance of his identity. This drink is the bringing together of many different parts, in order to create something beautiful—and delicious.

Enjoy while swapping some meaningful stories with someone you love.

~~~~~~~~~~~~~~~~~~~~~~~~~~~~~~~~~~~~~~~~~~~~~~~~~~~

### INGREDIENTS

15 lime wedges

10 lemon wedges

5 orange wedges

10 tsp sugar

5 cups crushed ice

5 cups lemon soda water

### INSTRUCTIONS

1. In a pitcher, combine your washed lime, lemon, and orange wedges, and sugar.

2. Muddle the fruit until the juice is extracted.

3. Add your crushed ice and soda water to the pitcher.

4. Stir gently a few times.

**Note:** Makes about five servings.

# Ben-Stir

## BEN-HUR BY LEW WALLACE

~~~~~~~~~~~~~~~~~~~~~~~~~~~~~~~~~~~~~~~~~~~~~~~~~~~~~~~~~~~

If "simplicity is perfection," consider this one perfect because it's as simple as it gets, with only two ingredients (okay, I guess one ingredient would technically be the simplest, but we have to keep things interesting).

This simple, epic beverage has a pink hue—symbolic of Iris's beauty in the film, and so tasty that your "cups of happiness" will be anything but "empty."

Get ready, because your gathering is about to be "Bigger than *Ben-Hur*!"

~~~~~~~~~~~~~~~~~~~~~~~~~~~~~~~~~~~~~~~~~~~~~~~~~~~~~~~~~~~

## INGREDIENTS

½ pitcher of ice

5 cups grapefruit juice

5 cups soda water

5 sprigs of rosemary for garnish

## INSTRUCTIONS

1. Fill a pitcher with ice.

2. Add in the grapefruit juice and soda water. Give it a few stirs.

3. Pour into glasses, and garnish each with a sprig of rosemary.

**Note:** Makes about five servings.

# Taming of the Screwdriver

## *THE TAMING OF THE SHREW* BY WILLIAM SHAKESPEARE

Loosely based on this play by Shakespeare, *10 Things I Hate About You*, or what we like to call around here, *10 Things I Drank About You*, has one tiny little difference—Kat Stratford and Patrick Verona are actually in love, unlike their Shakespearean counterparts.

This take on a typical Screwdriver incorporates orange (Kat's wonderfully sour demeanor), soda water (Bianca's effervescence), an orange twist (the boys' twisted arrangement behind the girls' backs), and a little dash of heavenly coconut milk (the perfect ending).

### INGREDIENTS

½ pitcher of ice

½ pitcher freshly squeezed orange juice

¼ pitcher coconut milk

⅓ pitcher soda water

Orange twists for garnish

### INSTRUCTIONS

1. Fill a pitcher with ice.

2. Add in your orange juice and coconut milk. Stir one or two times.

3. Top off with your soda water. Give it a gentle stir.

4. Pour into glasses.

5. Garnish each with an orange twist.

**Note:** Makes about five servings.

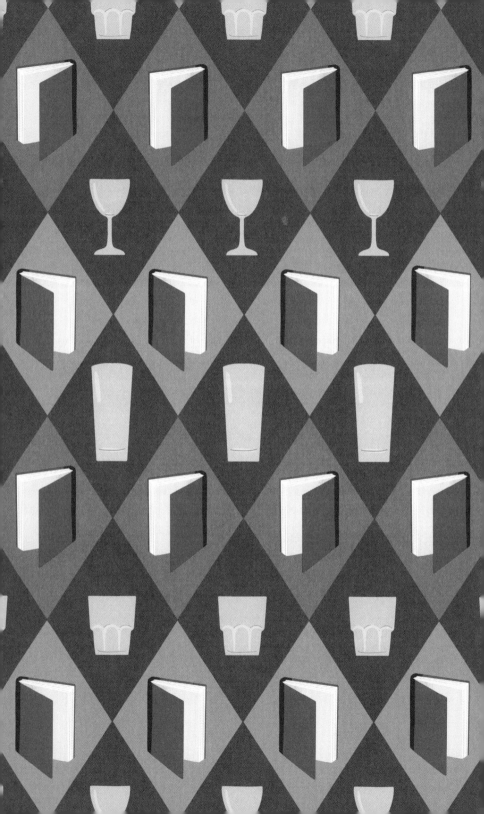

# The Sober Games

No alcohol? No problem. Beer pong has nothing on these party games. All the fun, without the hangover. Cheers!

## The Dialogue

They say writing is asking great questions. This activity is like twenty-one questions, except you have to answer each hot q in under five seconds.

1. Every player has to write out ten questions, and throw them into a jar, basket, or Mark Twain-esque top hat.

2. Each player pulls a question and must share the first answer that comes to their mind. (Answer within five seconds!)

3. Take turns until you answer twenty-one questions as a group.

Write your own rule for how to determine a winner (and a grand prize).

# Imagery

If a picture's worth a thousand words, get ready to drum up a novel's worth of act-outs. It's charades, but every answer is a book title.

1.  The players split into two teams.

2.  Each team generates fifteen book titles and throws them into their team jar, basket, or a hat that only Zora Neale Hurston could pull off.

3.  Taking turns, one member of each team pulls a book title from the other team's container and acts out clues for their teammates. Teams get ninety seconds to guess the book title.

Rather play a Pictionary-esque game? Or what we like to call around here, "Illustration?" The same rules apply; just draw the clues instead.


# The Climax

Just like the climax of any story, this can be the most exciting part of your day, week, or...life? Like "f*ck, marry, kill," but you have to decide which literary characters (or authors) you want to bang, betroth, or bury.

1.  Give Player One a list of three literary characters and/or authors to whom they must assign bang, betroth, or bury.

2.  They *must* explain their reasoning—the more detail, the better! Then, they get to pick three for the next player.

3.  The winner is the one who makes the best decisions based on character backstories, or other fun facts.

## Narrative(s)

This game gives a whole new meaning to first, second, and third person. Like the game of telephone, but with writing!

1. Player One writes one sentence of a story and passes it to Player Two.

2. Player Two writes the second sentence of the story and passes it to the next player. Repeat until each player has written one line of the story.

3. Starting with Player One, guess what the player next to you (starting with Player Two) wrote. Whoever makes the most accurate guess wins!

## Satire

Never judge a book by its cover, but what about its title? Humor us, and yourselves, with this one—it's time to funnify some book titles!

1. Each player creates five funny titles based on books of their choice. Throw all the titles into a jar, basket, or iconic newsie cap à la Andy Sachs in *The Devil Wears Prada*.

2. Players take turns pulling a title and guessing "the author."

3. Get it right, go again! When all the titles are gone, the player with the highest amount of correct guesses wins.

## Antagonist

Although we're all the protagonists of our own story, you're the antagonist of this game. Like two truths and a lie, but with two lies and a truth. They say write what you know, but in this case, you'll write what you don't.

1.  Each player thinks of two lies and one truth to share with the other player(s) aloud.

2.  Each player writes down which fun fact they think is the speaker's truth.

3.  Once each player has shared their three things, tally up the votes to see who has the most correct answers.


## The Ending

If art is never finished, it's your turn to edit as you see fit. Ready for *your* happy ending?

1.  Each player rewrites the ending to the book of their choice.

2.  The group votes for their favorite rewrite.

3.  Winner gets to pick the next book everyone reads!

# Conclusion

Whether you're a teetotaler or you've been tee-totally sneaking vodka into every one of these recipes, we hope you channel your inner author and make these drinks your own.

Because, just like Toni Morrison said, "If there's a book that you want to read, but it hasn't been written yet, then you must write it." Well, that's how we feel about drinks. You're the creator of your own cup. Revise as needed, and revel in every sip!

Like your new favorite book, once you find a drink that you just can't put down, feel free to share it with your non-drinking buddies, plant-based pals, or the fellow literature lovers in your life.

And when you share what you're sipping, snap a photo with your MockTale and use #MockTales for a chance to be featured across our platforms!

# Acknowledgements

Writing this book has been such a fun (and tasty) journey. To everyone who has been a part of this project—whether through conversations, feedback, or encouragement—thank you, thank you, thank you.

A big shout out to the *Self-Helpless* podcast community for your support as we crawl in the direction of our dreams.

Thank you to Woz Flint for your early reads and edits to help "make it better," as you always do.

Thank you to Lucy Giller for the beautiful illustrations and layout of this book.

To the entire publishing team at Mango, thank you for bringing this book to life.

To all the incredible authors that made this book possible because you were brave enough to share your stories with the world.

Thank you to our friends and family, to whom we often said, "Here drink this!" and to our surprise, they did, with no questions asked.

Also—our husbands, Derek and Cam. You're very neat n' stuff.

And of course, our dogs, Winnie, Maverick, and Goose. Because with Dog, all things are possible.

# About the Authors

## Delanie Fischer

Delanie Fischer is a comedy writer, activist, and host of the top-rated podcast *Self-Helpless*, living in Los Angeles with her husband, Cam, and their rescued dogs, Maverick and Goose. You can keep up with Delanie at www.delaniefischer.com.

## Lindsey Smith

Lindsey Smith is an author, publisher, and bookstore owner living in Pennsylvania with her punk rock husband and their beloved dog, Winnie. You can keep up with Lindsey at www.TheLindseySmith.com.

Mango Publishing, established in 2014, publishes an eclectic list of books by diverse authors—both new and established voices—on topics ranging from business, personal growth, women's empowerment, LGBTQ studies, health, and spirituality to history, popular culture, time management, decluttering, lifestyle, mental wellness, aging, and sustainable living. We were named 2019 and 2020's #1 fastest growing independent publisher by Publishers Weekly. Our success is driven by our main goal, which is to publish high-quality books that will entertain readers as well as make a positive difference in their lives.

Our readers are our most important resource; we value your input, suggestions, and ideas. We'd love to hear from you—after all, we are publishing books for you!

Please stay in touch with us and follow us at:

Facebook: Mango Publishing

Twitter: @MangoPublishing

Instagram: @MangoPublishing

LinkedIn: Mango Publishing

Pinterest: Mango Publishing

Newsletter: mangopublishinggroup.com/newsletter

Banned books are bold, provocative, and sometimes burned—making them extra hot, just like these mocktails. One sip and you'll immediately know why they are sometimes forbidden. Yes, they are THAT good. Make a serving to share with your next book club. Come to discuss the pages, stay to enjoy the beverages.